Buds will be roses,
and kittens, cats.

— PROVERB

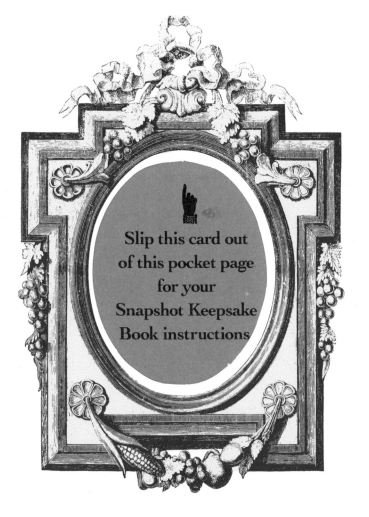

Slip this card out
of this pocket page
for your
Snapshot Keepsake
Book instructions

My Cat

Designed and produced by Marquand Books, Inc.
Quality printing and binding by Tien Wah Press Pte, Ltd.,
977 Bukit Timah Road, Singapore 2158

Efforts have been made to find the copyright
holders of material used in this publication. We apologize for
any omissions or errors and will be pleased to include the
appropriate acknowledgments in future editions.

"Taffy Topaz" from *Songs for a Little House* by Christopher
Morley. Copyright 1917; copyright renewed 1945
by Christopher Morley. Reprinted by permission of
HarperCollins Publishers.

Sources for excerpts are:
"The Cat's Nursery" and "I Gave My Puss a Macaroon"
from *Baby Days*, Scribner and Company, 1877; "Dinah," by
Norman Gale, from *Poetry's Plea for Animals*, Lothrop, Lee, and
Shepard, 1927; "The Gardener's Cat," by Patrick R.
Chalmers, from *The Cat in Verse*, Little, Brown, and Co., 1935;
"Mrs. Pussy's Dinner," by Emilie Poulsson, from *Finger Plays
for Nursery and Kindergarten*, D. Lothrop Co., 1893.

ISBN 0-87701-852-9

Distributed in Canada by Raincoast Books
112 East 3rd Avenue, Vancouver, B.C. V5T1C8

1 3 5 7 9 10 8 6 4 2

Chronicle Books
275 Fifth Street, San Francisco, California 94103

# My Cat

A
SNAPSHOT
KEEPSAKE
BOOK

MICHELE DURKSON CLISE

CHRONICLE BOOKS
San Francisco

If man could be crossed with the cat,
it would improve man,
but deteriorate the cat.

— MARK TWAIN

# Vita

My name is

_____

I belong to

_____

_____

I live at

_____

_____

_____

I was born

_____

My license number is

_____

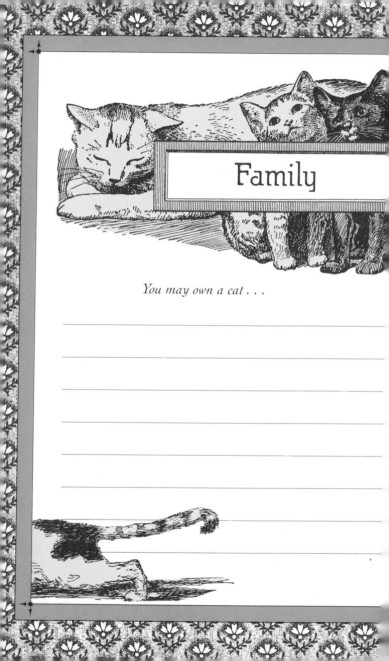

# Family

*You may own a cat . . .*

# History

*but cannot govern one.*

# Clever Things I Do

_____

_____

_____

_____

_____

_____

_____

_____

# Taffy Topaz

Taffy, the topaz-colored cat,
Thinks now of this and now of that,
But chiefly of his meals.
Asparagus, and cream, and fish,
Are objects of his Freudian wish;
What you don't give, he steals.

His gallant heart is strongly stirred
By clink of plate or flight of bird,
He has a plumy tail;
At night he treads on stealthy pad
As merry as Sir Galahad
A-seeking of the Grail.

His amiable amber eyes
Are very friendly, very wise;
Like Buddha, grave and fat,
He sits, regardless of applause,
And thinking, as he kneads his paws,
What fun to be a cat!

— CHRISTOPHER MORLEY

### Who is to bell the cat?

The well-known fable tells of a cunning old mouse who suggested that the mice hang a bell on the cat's neck to warn them of her approach. "Excellent," said a wise young mouse, "but who will undertake the job?"

*The cat is a lion to the mouse.*

—ALBANIAN PROVERB

# Mrs. Pussy's Dinner

Mrs. Pussy, sleek and fat,
With her kittens four,
Went to sleep upon the mat
By the kitchen door.

MRS. PUSSY
(Right hand)

KITTENS FOUR

UPON THE MAT

UP SHE JUMPED

Mrs. Pussy heard a noise —
Up she jumped in glee:
"Kittens, maybe that's a mouse!
Let us go and see!"

Creeping, creeping, creeping on,
Silently they stole;
But the little mouse had gone
Back within its hole.

WITHIN ITS HOLE

"Well," said Mrs. Pussy then,
  "To the barn we'll go;
We shall find the swallow there
  Flying to and fro."

So the cat and kittens four
  Tried their very best;
But the swallows flying fast
  Safely reached the nest!

NEST

Home went hungry Mrs. Puss
  And her kittens four;
Found their dinner on a plate
  By the kitchen door.

PLATE

As they gathered round the plate,
  They agreed 'twas nice
That it could not run away
  Like the birds and mice!

— EMILIE POULSSON

# What I Like

*The cat loves fish . . .*

# What I Dislike

*but does not like to wet her paws.*
— ENGLISH PROVERB

I gave my puss a macaroon,
And bade her eat with a silver spoon;
I brought a glass of sparkling wine,
And bade the pretty creature dine.

But see what came of it, a-lack!
That naughty pussy turned her back;
Now wasn't it a dreadful sight
To see a puss so impolite?

Doctor Johnson used to go out and buy oysters
for his famous Hodge, because the servants resented
such an errand, and he wished the servants to
be friendly toward the cat.

Pussy cat, Pussy cat, where have you been?
I've been to London to look at the Queen.

Pussy cat, Pussy cat, what did you there?
I frightened a little mouse under the chair.

— NURSERY RHYME

miew, miew, miew

A cat came fiddling out of a barn,
With a pair of bagpipes under her arm;
She could sing nothing but fiddle cum fee,
The mouse has married the bumble bee.

— NURSERY RHYME

# Friends

_____

_____

_____

_____

_____

_____

_____

"If you want to know the character of a man
find out what his cat thinks of him."

— ANONYMOUS

# Cats around

Bulgarian *kotki*

Chinese *mao*

Danish *kat*

Finnish *kissa*

French *chat*

German *katze*

Greek *catta*

Hindi *billi*

Icelandic *köttur*

# the World

Italian  *gatto*

Japanese  *neko*

Persian  *gorbe*

Russian  *koshka*

Spanish  *gato*

Swahili  *paka*

Swedish  *katt*

Thai  *maew*

Turkish  *kedi*

The cat's a saint while there are no mice about.

— JAPANESE PROVERB

# The Cat's Nursery

Mrs. Puss found her kittens so much in the way
She made them a nursery where they could play,
And told both the nurses to keep the kits quiet,
And send them to bed if they made any riot.

"Go find your mittens,
you silly kittens.
And be quick about it too!"
Miew, miew, miew, miew.
Miew, miew, miew, miew.

"What! found your mittens,
    You darling kittens,
Then you shall have some pie."
    Purr, purr, purr, purr.
    Purr, purr, purr, purr.

No matter how much the cats fight,
there always seem to be plenty of kittens.

—ABRAHAM LINCOLN

# Dinah

Our Dinah is a Persian cat
Too beautiful for words!
She wears about her neck a bell
To warn the garden birds.

Her eyes are blue as thrushes' eggs,
Her coat is brown as cloves,
And when she's wakeful, in my lap
She kneads her little loaves.

If you could see how diligent
Her paws are when they knead,
You'd think she had at least a score
Of kittycats to feed.

And often, lying in my lap,
So velvety and still,
With steadiness she grinds and grinds
A little coffee mill.

To hear the lovely miller grind,
To watch her knead, is sweet;
It makes me want to pick her up
To kiss her face and feet.

I love her sleeping in the sun,
A hot and silky bale;
I love her when she tries to pounce
Upon her shadow's tail.

— NORMAN GALE

Grave scholars and mad lovers all admire
And love, and each alike, at his full tide

Those suave and puissant cats, the fireside's pride,
Who like the sedentary life and glow of fire.

— CHARLES BAUDELAIRE

# The Gardener's Cat

The gardener's cat's called Mignonette,
She hates the cold, she hates the wet,
She sits among the hothouse flowers
And sleeps for hours and hours and hours.

She dreams she is a tiger fierce
With great majestic claws that pierce,
She sits by the hot-water pipes
And dreams about a coat of stripes;

And in her slumbers she will go
And stalk the sullen buffalo,
And when he roars across the brake
She does not wink, she does not wake.

It must be perfectly immense
To dream with such magnificence,
And pass the most inclement day
In this indeed stupendous way.

She dreams of India's sunny clime,
And only wakes at dinnertime,
And even then she does not stir
But waits till milk is brought to her.

How nice to be the gardener's cat,
She troubles not for mouse or rat,
But, when it's coming down in streams,
She sits among the flowers and dreams.

The gardener's cat would be the thing,
Her dreams are so encouraging;
She dreams that she's a tiger, yet
She's just a cat called Mignonette!

— PATRICK R. CHALMERS

# Medical Records

Vet's name and telephone

_____

_____

Allergies

_____

_____

_____

_____

Special medications

Vaccinations

# Sitter's Instructions

_____

_____

_____

_____

_____

_____

_____

In case of an emergency

_____

_____

_____

_____